More praise for *Now Calls Me Daughter*

Some refer to Alzheimer's as a journey; Christine Jones knows that it is at least as much a place. Whether you have lived in the land of dementia disease or not, this astonishing book serves as a sharply-observed guide through that territory's emotional dynamism. Each poem's particulars are as delightful as they are devastating, mirroring the reality of the disease. There is no looking away, but you don't want to. — **Melanie Braverman**, Author of *Red* (Perugia Press, 2002), Co-founder, Alzheimer's Family Support Center

Now Calls Me Daughter is a tender dedication to a matriarch who is losing her memory. Jones gets honest with direct addresses to her, "I am your daughter/more glaring each year…" and "Mother sing me/into what comes next". Yet there are also narratives written in the third person simulating the distancing that happens with dementia while also making her mother more universal for the reader, "While her body rises/out of its slender girl" and "Calls me in the middle of the night/to say voices are watching her sleep". Jones created erasures from a dementia- related behaviors guidebook, though superimposed neurons obstruct the language for the reader not unlike language for one with memory loss. — **Kevin McLellan**, author of *In other words you*, and *Ornitheology*

Now Calls Me Daughter

Christine Jones

Nixes Mate Books
Allston, Massachusetts

Copyright © 2022 Christine Jones

Book design by d'Entremont

Cover photograph used with permission.

All rights reserved. This book or any portion thereof may not be reproduced or used in any manner whatsoever without the express written permission of the publisher except for the use of brief quotations in a book review or scholarly journal.

ISBN 978-1-949279-43-6

Nixes Mate Books
POBox 1179
Allston, MA 02134
nixesmate.pub

For Mom

Overcome space, and all we have left is Here.
　　Overcome time, and all we have left is Now.
　　　　Richard Bach, *Jonathan Livingston Seagull*

Contents

Tea Ceremony	3
Hard to Imagine Birds Dying of Old Age	4
Now Calls Me Daughter	5
Now	6
Now in Autumn: Sonnet I	7
What I Want to Say Driving Home After My Mother's Check-Up	8
After the Move	11
To the Larger Pile Decaying	12
Now in Autumn: Sonnet II	13
Dear Bella	14
I AM SO GLAD YOU ARE HERE Spell the Felt Letters on Burlap Hanging from a Dowel on Our Bathroom Wall	15
The Hostess Packs for Assisted Living	17
My Mother Asks Me to Write Her a Poem About the Sky	18
This, Too, Shall Pass	19
It's the Middle of the Night	20
On Wednesdays at Ocean State Job Lot	21
My Eighty-Six-Year-Old Father Falls	22
My Mother Advocates for Her Dad Who's Been Dead Thirty-Seven Years	23
Excerpts from My Father's Late-Night Emails	24
On Their 63rd Wedding Anniversary	25

Wondering Who I'll Be in My Mother's Newest Script for
    "Let Me Introduce You to My One Hundred and
        Twenty-Year-Old Father"   26
On Tuesdays Mom Comes with Me to Deliver Meals on Wheels   28
When the Sun Goes Down   29
My Father Spends His Days Missing Her   30
Not a Bird   31
Ignoring the Mortals   34
Then   35
Follow the Tributaries   36
On Cape Cod Bay   37
I Love You Big Like the Sky, But Actually   38
Self-Portrait Thirty Years from Now   39
ن   40
Fine   41
At Youville Place   42
I Choose to Publish My Love for You   43
Then   44
Plaques & Tangles   45
Mother's Day   46

Now Calls Me Daughter

Tea Ceremony

My mother's wrist bends just so,
and the Staffordshire teapot tips
a flawless stream into her cup.
The cat she no longer ushers off,
sleuths his tail between the rim
and handle, then settles his stripes
on the counter to stare down the jay
picking at the suet cake. The stereo
replays *La Vie en Rose*, the cat
pretending stillness,
gingersnaps poised on a plate.
The kitchen's stool urges me
upright. My mother reopens
the cupboard, refolds
the checkered napkin, picks
lint off her lilac sweater.

Hard to Imagine Birds Dying of Old Age

The garland of robins on her magnolia tree –

the thing she says she'll miss the most
when she's gone. The birds delight

for hours. One day,
I trim the branches but cut

too much. She cries. The sun.
Now, a chance to leaven the raisin bread.

Mom, let's sing that song,
Plaisir d'amour, again.

Now Calls Me Daughter

Calls me in the middle of the night
to say voices are watching her sleep.
She's looking for her shoes; she's
watched the nightly news, feels
the flooding in Japan just outside
her bedroom door.

I bring her closer, nearer
the sun's blaze & vanishing.

She sits habitually in her blue chair.
A hummingbird siphons the sugar.
She sings, in French, a song I don't know
about a warm embrace. Now
dices ripe tomatoes for the sauce
I'm simmering with Merlot.

Now

She hugs

and she's right

here.

Here.

In this hug.

She's alright.

She is, right?

Here,

in her hug?

Now in Autumn: Sonnet I

Each day she takes the leaves that fall.
Her favorite flowered gloves grab hold
the small shrub rake – she clears them all.
Now waits for me. I'm there, she hopes,

by half past nine. She's at the door,
a beacon in her berry fleece.
Does she wonder who she's waiting for.
And the spray of pink crepe myrtle keeps

co-mingling with the mulch & slate.
Lost in her plant-watering ritual,
she doesn't notice that I'm late –
she's talking kindly to a squirrel.

And from the fence I see and hear
her, stooped down low, say Come, *ma chère*.

What I Want to Say Driving Home After My Mother's Check-Up

The audiologist adjusts her headphones,
tells her to repeat:

Say Talk *Talk*
Say Hard *Hard*
Say Dog *Dog*
Say Bite ___

Say Call *Call*
Say Net *Net*

...

It's okay.   It's what we become;

a sepia tone I've seen fall
across Utah's red rock –

striations glowing, baring those layers
polished by grim and pitiless erosion.

...

What we fear is travelling toward us.
But so is what we love; what is good,
and tender. You are my mother,

more palpable each day. You
reminisce, tell me again (dare I say)
of Mr. and Mrs. Honeybloom, your first apartment,
pushing the stroller downtown, and of when
I was young, in the backseat, hugging your shoulders
while you drove, we sang
take me home, country roads.

I am your daughter,
more glaring each year; my words
slipping, too, like the sleep
that doesn't come, or
the morning paper. I'm missing
your affirmative singular dots, all the while

my own ellipses pile, weightless thoughts.
Dear words, (Mom let's pray):
Brave this mouth serrated, its grave
doubt.   Scars are acceptable.

…

The fog persists. Meaning
anything I say is questionable.

Heavy mist forges my lines.
How to be understood?

A rattled burst of air strews
a small opening in the windshield,
enough, so if hunched
with chin jutted, I can spot
the exit sign in time.

After the Move

We sort through a box full of shoes.
My size, Mom says, wondering
how they got there. She unfolds
the checked blue blanket,
My favorite color. How'd you know?

I know she likes anything blue, also
a crucifix in her kitchen, even if it is
next to a holiday wreath on this warm day in June.

She offers her ice cream bar
shaped like Mickey Mouse.

She bites one ear. I bite the other.

To the Larger Pile Decaying

Now aims her life to be all-purposeful,
like flour, like a cleaning agent, like
the perfect black dress she would wear
to an interview and, also, a funeral.

She handwashes her socks, she mops,
then paces the kitchen floor. Makes muffins
from a box while pantry moths hover.
Burnt edges. She adjusts.

Now gathers crumbs, throws
them outside on the hedges
for cheeky sparrows. And more
leaves to tidy from behind the back door.

Now in Autumn: Sonnet II

On the clothesline, dries her flowered blouse.
And while a taut breeze blows, she makes
precise small piles by the house.
No leaf escapes her merry rake.

Now wears a berry fleece, wool hat,
ill-fitted, knitted long ago.
She fancies red birds bright & fat,
spreads toasted breadcrumbs in the grove.

Now greets the cedar tree by name,
the cat, the squirrel, with *ma chère*.
Her thoughts, unfazed, a late noon shade,
rest in the old oak rocking chair.

And when the tree-frog hours come,
she briefly hears her name, *Maintenant*.

Dear Bella

I maneuver you into this cardboard box
that will carry you back
to the shelter where two weeks ago
you seemed the perfect *minou* for mom to love
because she worries if the voice she hears
at the foot of her bed is that of her husband,
her father, or the neighbor building his shed.
Every day she wipes your pee with a small towel,
washes it in bleach on a large load setting. She
wants to hold you tightly & always.
How can she not be attached.
Even when you scratch.
When you bite. I'm sorry Bella,
none of this feels right.

I AM SO GLAD YOU ARE HERE Spell the Felt Letters on Burlap Hanging from a Dowel on Our Bathroom Wall

So you'll see it says my mother when
        I object, embarrassed
by the handcrafted letters. Afraid
        they'd curl,   then fall
chartreuse & yellow, onto my thighs, slip
      through the chubby crack,
          bring attention to the weirdness
      of blood & sponge.

         I remember probing
    with the cardboard tube, trying
      to find the opening;   a teenager exposed,
     sweating over a porcelain bowl.

          Later,
at a roadside bar in Rishikesh, I must aim for a hole
          dug in the dirt behind a low,
    crumbling wall teeming with flies & trash
 while remote men lean
         against sultry brick.

Now I know.   Not every girl has a clean facility.
    Not every girl knows her mother.

Now, I appreciate the blood,

                its birth & breath & my mother
holding my face repeating.

The Hostess Packs for Assisted Living

She'll have no kitchen; no stove-top,
only the hot pot. Yet the drop-leaf
will be lifted, the floral tablecloth spread,
and biscuits will flourish
on white scalloped plates.
There'll be ginger tea in matching cups.

Now's packing the whole ten-piece
setting. Just in case.

My Mother Asks Me to Write Her a Poem About the Sky

She wants to brag to her new assisted-living friend. She, who loves me *big like the sky*, who tells me *look up* when I'm in need of a prayer. She can't know I'm lost & starless in Delhi where there's a cow at every turn. Where a girl knocks on my car window. Can I learn to carry bricks on my head? A bushel of hay? I count each day in sugar crystals & fennel seeds. Underwater in a pool, the only place I can breathe – the world is smaller than it is. Far, too far from home, she can't hear the city chant its six million hymns.

This, Too, Shall Pass

is what you said Sunday,
over the phone from your small
room where all meals are lukewarm
and half-pint milk cartons
collect in the mini fridge.

is what you say, is
what you always say
in times like these, except now
to be positive means
something negative, means
you cannot leave & don't know
if Delores, your friend, will be okay,
means hours of Solitaire, visits on Zoom,
your nightgown worn late into the afternoon.

But *notice the daffodils*, you'd also say.
Their abundance. And *look at the herring run*.

Your appetite has passed, and so has your prayer,
giving way to sleep. You,
in a hospital room, tired of tests, of tubes,

as if you didn't miss
the goldfinch on the thistle.
His jaunty lisp.

It's the Middle of the Night

The dog knows better
which way in the darkness to go

& pulls your sleepless son toward the edges
where the soft ivy grows. Meanwhile your

mother's wandering just a few miles away, looking
for her purse, her coat, her most comfortable shoes.

You ask yourself, *if I let go, what then?*
Your son is missing, and

your mother's already gone.
In the still-dark hours

the great horned owl probes.
The cotton sheet's too chilly, the coverlet's

too warm. You keep your eyelids closed,
feel the cedar tree's shadow, the dog

at the foot of your bed curled tight.
You lie awake with one leg out, alert to

the shifting, how it records itself by light.

On Wednesdays at Ocean State Job Lot

She adds, too, a collar for the cat
she used to have, a small frying pan
for the crepes she used to make, and
another red sweater for the holidays.
Aisle 6, she's rummaging
through her desk. Aisle 8?
She's looking for her father's
address. Here? Now? She reads
her list of neat penmanship.

My Eighty-Six-Year-Old Father Falls

Weeks after they moved,
        Dad went missing
        in her mind.

    What does anyone know

        of tangled filaments,
        of clustered bits of beta-amelyoid,
        of savvy caregiving,   of improvisation,

of sixty-two years of marriage,
              of pints of whiskey,

of a father struggling from a floor,
a swelling bump on his head.

My Mother Advocates for Her Dad Who's Been Dead Thirty-Seven Years

Can Papa live here, too?
He never complains.

...

Voyons, Papa, no need to worry.

Excerpts from My Dad's Late-Night Emails

She won't accept that I am me.
This sure as hell isn't fun.
I'm *gone again*.
What will I do without your mom?
She says the cat's her *only friend*.
I'm *Papa*, now, who's here.
I've no idea how this works out.
Not ready for her to be in Memory Care.
Been demoted to the living room couch.
Why does *he* get to stay?
She wants the truth; I tell her – *your dad is dead*.
I don't know what else to say.
Miss my comforter, my warm bed.
We read God's Prayer for the Anxious.
Please, I ask, pray for us.
She won't accept that I am me.

On Their 63rd Wedding Anniversary

Like a common gull on the rail
my father sits beside her.
They talk about the whale
that once surfaced & rolled,
how it exposed its thick-lidded eye.
Today, she connects
waves & wind & her life with him
for the first time
in three rough years.
Tinged-pink sky, soft
as his hand on hers, curls
with the tide.

If only in their sleep tonight, they could die.

The waning moon
sketches their evening flats.
Not quite the hermit crab's trailing
but a map nonetheless.

Wondering Who I'll Be in My Mother's Newest Script for "Let Me Introduce You to My One Hundred and Twenty-Year-Old Father"

I can be, maybe,
ma tante Fleurette from
Quebec, wearing pale
blue shoes, quilting ladies
with peach hats. I'll have
white peppermints in a bowl,
though I won't know
how to pretend
her polio. Better if
      I'm *ma tante* Carmelle,
      the Franciscan
      who traveled
      the world. I'll read
      to orphaned children
      in Rome, canoe with
      the Inuits of Manitoba.
Or I can be *ma tante* Reine, the nun
who dwells in the convent by a pond
where ducks feast on leftover ends
of unholy host.
I'll mend days sewing hems
of sisters' habits. It

       won't be that bad –
       I'll smile and nod, say
       pardon? Mom
will expect I can't hear,
will repeat her stories
about Mr. & Mrs. Honeybloom,
and
the hand-me-downs she had to wear –
thirteenth child. Or with luck
I'll stay
       Christine – she'll know
       my voice, she'll know
the birthmark on my right cheek

On Tuesdays Mom Comes with Me to Deliver Meals on Wheels

She sits in the passenger seat with Dotty, my white terrier, shedding on her navy-blue pants while I knock on doors –

    J. hangs a stocking all year round.

    T. wears the same striped sweater each week.

    A. may or may not be home

    D. invites me in for tea

    R. asks me my name again.

    S. struts his American flag pajama pants.

    E. writes me a poem.

    L. & L. chime in unison.

When the Sun Goes Down

I make Don's egg over-easy with a slice of ham when he's here.
We take our daily walk, climb the hill, if we can, near here.

I read the morning *Globe*, enjoy the cove's view.
He talks to the neighbor who lives around here.

We sit on the couch, eat chips and clementines, watch CNN.
News about our children, grand, and great-grand, we wait to hear.

I've been forgetting. It's normal. So's my loss of taste and smell.
Last night I almost fell. Heard a strange man's voice. Who's here?

The other day, my dad appeared, but where the hell is Don?
The one in the picture. Why is he not here?

Don's back but Papa's gone. He doesn't know this town.
Bon dieu! Don's left again. Goddamn it, he's not here.

Papa keeps me company. He never complains.
I take the neurological exam. Both Dad and Don are here.

I, Rachel, daughter of Raoul, wife of Don, say my prayers.
St. Anthony, help me. I won't sleep with just any man who's here.

My Father Spends His Days Missing Her

Hangs a hummingbird feeder.

Doesn't know
if they'll fly
this high up.

Not a Bird

Mom, it isn't. Even before you
repeated yourself & your days,
before you taught me to say grace,
time was never a bird.

Rather, it's the bread you throw
for the sparrow, that lands on the hedges,
the raw slide of an oyster, sandflats'
figure lines, loamy blooms, my strand of hair
in the shower stall, a green-eyed girl
in Delhi knocking on our dusty Subaru.
Sugar crystals & fennel seeds,
brailled bark & pickled beets
from the foothills of Wyoming,
far from the right whale's spray
& the sunlight's cross on the dune
shack's door; the world
redeeming itself, revealing
a small hole in the screen.

It's the blue eggshell in the lawn,
the habitual piles you make
with your flowered gloves & merry
rake, the lemon gelato melting
on the nightstand, roses

in a jelly jar. And the olive oil
we sipped from a farm in Crete.
Are you back there, Mom, with the goats
bleating in the gorge? Are you raining
down the mountain trail through
the scrub pines, or coursing the Seine
to the floating piscine?

I look for answers within hives
hanging from the eaves of the shed.
Another shovel, another wasp.
What or who gets to live?
The great horned owl probes. A mouse
in the trap, not quite dead.

Have you noticed the nest in the budding
crepe myrtle? Yes, we've been here
for quite a while. I forgive you,
my missed birthday un-penciled on the calendar
that still leans against your desk.

Time is not a bird. It's twelve pairs of swans
streaming in the cove. Your placid face
preserving their wake. It's the sea
glass found on shore, held
in a tiny terra cotta bowl. It's carved
on the bottom of a thrown-clay vase, or

marked with an X on a kid-drawn map.
It rides the bi-plane, changes
with easterly winds pivoting
the archangel statue mounted
on a cathedral wing. Can you hear
the choir's collected voices?

A bottle captures it
crossing an ocean, where a boy
finds it at low tide. O Time!
You will or will not hide
how we'll fare the loss
of a mother in her warm bed.

Ignoring the Mortals

She retreats
to the thinning
room turned
upside
down.
Her mind
a fig tree
in a Victorian robe,
a stranger
to the heavens.
Ill at ease
with the brush
of an osprey's wing.
She is planted
in the valley,
here. Not here.

Then

She played volleyball, almost
 became a nun. Never
  learned to swim, ice skate, or
 ride a bike. She floated in the pool lounge chair
  while we kids swam under, tipped her over.
She talked on a rotary phone with a cord not long enough
  to stop us fighting in the den. She shook
   the wooden spoon, instead, mouthed *Knock it off!*
She permed my hair, made me wear itchy wool.
  Wore zip-up boots. Gifted thank-you notes in stockings every year.
   Schooled us in etiquette & religious ed. She swore: *merde! mon dieu!*
    Walked twenty steps ahead.
  Wore berets & taught her grandkids *pommes, frais, bluets.*
She offered tea with ginger snaps. morning glory muffins,
  crepes, *nice* soups. She
rubbed our heads to help us sleep. Gave great bear
  hugs & green chocolate mints,
 kisses on each cheek.

Follow the Tributaries

Now's floating
on the pool's lounge chair,
sun rising under the blue loch
of her eye illuminating
a buoy or a duck?

She's wearing her Sunday best –
plum sweater & a gold cross around her neck.

On Cape Cod Bay

If I could see something in the cove
from the body of the swan, I might know
my mother's hours before sunrise,
wings doubled in the light. Here's the wake
where a NO WAKE buoy anchors, and she
wades in common minnows. If I could see
something other than her puzzled neck, I'd know
about her quiet inlet and I could topple
aging's cairn: restless homesteader
in her itchy brain. She confuses
her husband with her father.
I could empty her tiny tricycle of nuns,
keep her away from the pleasurable flesh
of corpses – their blank nametags shouting
Sr._____ – and doff dementia's white
stockings, the Virgin Mary under the tulip tree. Then she
could die, an old crone saying nothing more about the cove
with its split rivers – choppy, irreverent – far away
from the dunes, the single artery that led her to
her cottage, that held her to this peace. I wouldn't keep
her a minute longer. She could listen to the moon.

I Love You Big Like the Sky, But Actually
after "I love you to the moon &" by Chen Chen

I'd rather love you how the moon sets
over the cove. Not let love
get lost in the inescapable
blue. With you there
somewhere I can't see. The sky's
too big for the geranium pot, too far
from the marsh. I want you here,
in your old oak rocking chair,
my love, back & forth.

Self-Portrait Thirty Years from Now

They're not on my nightstand or desk.
A hassle. Nor in my striped purse.
Meg looks for my glasses and frets.
Oh help us, please, dear Universe –

I'm nearer the end. She's nearer the start.
On aging: Normal I was told.
My mother said so, crossed her heart,
us laughing, on the patio.

Like her, I clean the floors each day,
watch the sparrows in the hedges.
Like me, Meg swims in Skaket Bay;
eyes for sun in cold blue stretches.

We're making her favorite rhubarb pie.
In the pantry. My glasses. Half-smile. Sigh.
.

ن

"There, there waits the ark" by Kamelya Omayma Yousel

I see the ark, the Arabic letter,
as a winking emoji like
what my mother does after telling
a bad joke. Everything these days
turns into a mother poem.
There's something
about the ambiguous loss
of her compelling me
to write her in.
She occupies the
wingback chair. Last
week's paper reports
the missing girl she
says looks like me.

Fine

1.
We're fine.
It's fine.
From Old French *fin*.

The universe unspools its improvisational sweaters,
loose & uncomfortable.
I'm fine.

Pale polish, chipped & overdue, she moisturizes her cuticles.
Back & forth.
Back & forth.
Everything's fine!

She'd leave if only
Don/Dad/God would appear.

2.
Today, it's me
wet Bean boots on the basement steps.
My scream lands hard on concrete.

3.
Far away, in her rocker she sips crème de menthe, extra ice.
I'm on my couch with ice on my tailbone.

How long must we stay?

At Youville Place

Despite the fisher cats,
this chair is her field.

She rests under the bright canopy
and its low conversation makes her open

her fist, release. My mother
is common, a quiet dinner

growing quieter in her black purse.
Her compact mirror content with dreaming

of how to dream about something
while her body rises

out of its slender girl.
The one she heard for years

far from moonlight, boxed and awake.
A polished rock in the dirt of the field.

I Choose to Publish My Love for You

Upon news of this book he texts *it's a family matter*, suggests *wait until she's gone*. Between the lines; *she'd be pissed*. Mom, you might be upset at the attention toward anything amiss. You never liked being corrected. (Who does – It was Mr. Coffee, not Mr. Rogers, *thumb* tack, not *tum* tack. It was you who painted that vase of flowers in activities class). You are private; also what is true, light under a heavy-leafed canopy. Dear Mom, remember how we hooked our swinging legs from the bench under the brightening?

Then

We'd go to church midweek. Later, she sorted donated clothes at the rectory while I searched the candy bowls. Back home, we'd build pyramids of green beans, covet the tv, roll bologna & cheese. We'd play hide & seek while waiting for my siblings to get off the long yellow bus. She'd hug them, then continue her search for me in the trees.

Plaques & Tangles

   The day I was born you had a fever
     and the umbilical cord was wrapped
around my neck.
   You waited weeks
    to hold me to your breast.
        Now clustered & knotted
    proteins strangle you. You
sometimes call me Megan or Helen
       though you named me after Christ the Lord.
    You stand on the threshold,
 taking off your coat.   Oh hark
    mother   sing me
into what comes next.

Mother's Day

By the old duck shack in Nauset's east dune,
a gray sun shadows a cross on the door.
Two peeling Adirondack chairs marooned.

No one collects the driftwood from the shore.
Three pompous clouds, past noon, a shift
of a right whale's far-off spume spraying

droplets, millions. And I, shivering, bereft,
spill more. Distanced from my swaying
mother, here atop this windswept crest.

She, too, voyages home in her black church shoes.
And I, ankle deep in the throes,
keep watch as she, shimmering, goes.

Acknowledgements

cagibi "It's the Middle of the Night"

Hard Work of Hope Series from Massachusetts Poetry: "This, Too, Shall Pass"

Lily Poetry Review: "Neurons: A Series of Erasure*: mother, life happens, Let yourself sink, and a scene will repeat*

MSU Libraries Short Edition on Home and MSU's annual *Filmetry Festival, 2022*: "My Mother Asks Me to Write Her a Poem About the Sky for Mother's Day"

Nixes Mate Review's *Anthology In the Time of Covid,*: "My Eighty-Six-Year-Old Father Falls" (an earlier version)

On the Seawall: "Now Calls Me Daughter", "To the Larger Pile Decaying", "Now in Autumn: Sonnet I" Neurons: A Series of Erasure: *pictures in the album, There are limits, and this. Being*

Passengers Journal: "I AM SO GLAD YOU ARE HERE Spell the Felt Letters on Burlap Hanging from a Dowel on Our Bathroom Wall"

Résonance: "Now in Autumn: Sonnet II"

SWWIM Every Day: "My Mother Asks Me to Write Her a Poem About the Sky for Mother's Day" and "This, Too, Shall Pass"

Sugar House Review: "At Youville Place" and "ت"

Notes

According to the National Institute on Aging, Alzheimer's is a brain disorder that slowly destroys memory and thinking skills, and it's estimated that over six million Americans struggle with dementia as a result. My eighty-three-year-old mother has become part of this statistic. It's a wild disease in that it is unpredictable, like a feral cat or small child. Also, in the way it progresses, like weeds growing untamed and tangled. Poetry helped me give structure to the chaos. My writing became consumed with how to express the many emotions wrapped around all of us involved. Fortunately for my family, there are mostly good days and my mother's gracious and vibrant spirit persists.

"Ignoring the Mortals" inspired by Linda Gregg's "Hearing the Gods"

"At Youville Place" inspired by Linda Gregg's "How the Joy of it Was Used Up Long Ago"

"On Cape Cod Bay" inspired by Lynn Emanuel's "Inventing Father in Las Vegas"

In Gratitude

Thank you to Eileen Cleary for her insightful consideration, helping me shape my manuscript from its inception to this heartfelt collection. Thank you to Kevin McLellan for providing guidance and careful readings of these poems along the way, and to Melanie Braverman for her time and contribution. Many thanks to my poetry collectives: the Wild Geraniums, the Paper Tigresses, and Kevin McLellan's workshops. These poems emerged and then evolved with all those caring hawk eyes on them. And thank you to Michael McInnis and Annie Pluto at Nixes Mate for believing in this manuscript and designing a book to match its heart. Lastly, my love to Michael, Megs, and Owen for their everlasting love and support, and to my parents Don and Rachel, for modeling how to live with humility, grace, and gratitude.

About the Author

Christine Jones lives on Cape Cod, with her husband, where you'll find them swimming and running along its shores. She earned her MFA from Lesley University in Cambridge, Massachusetts, and is a therapist and mother of two. She's the author of *Girl Without a Shirt* (Finishing Line Press, 2020) and co-editor of the anthology, *Voices Amidst the Virus: Poets Respond to the Pandemic* (Lily Poetry Review Books, 2020). She's also the founder/editor-in-chief of *Poems2go* and associate editor of *Lily Poetry Review*. Her poetry can be found in numerous journals and anthologies in print and online

RECENT TITLES

FROM NIXES MATE

Dog-Walking In The Shadow Of Pyongyang · Devon Balwit

Truth and Other Lies · Pris Campbell

2 a.m. With Keats · Eileen Cleary

lesser case · Mark Decarteret

Series · Mari Deweese

Now Calls Me Daughter · Christine Jones

The Half-Said Things · Miriam O'Neal

Unfoldings · Clara Eugenia Ronderos

Banana Bread · J.D. Scimgeour

Nike Adjusting Her Sandal · Anastasia Vassos

FLY COTTON CHAPBOOK SERIES

The Passion of John Eliot · Michael McInnis

Chernobyl · Anne Pluto

Torero · Gloria Monaghan

Dear Teilhard, · Hannah Larrabee

Lose Sight of Heaven · Zofia Provizor

Innocents · Cindy Veech

In the Year of Ferraro · Jennifer Martelli

To receive a free copy (pay only $3 for 1st Class shipping, USA only) of Christine's chapbook, *Neurons: A Series of Erasure Poems*, go to https://nixes-mate.pub/product/neurons-a-series-of-erasure-poems-christine-jones/. During checkout type **Neurons** in the "Have a coupon…" box at the top of the page.

42° 19' 47.9" N 70° 56' 43.9" W

Nixes Mate is a navigational hazard in Boston Harbor used during the colonial period to gibbet and hang pirates and mutineers.

Nixes Mate Books features small-batch artisanal literature, created by writers who use all 26 letters of the alphabet and then some, honing their craft the time-honored way: one line at a time.

nixesmate.pub

www.ingramcontent.com/pod-product-compliance
Lightning Source LLC
Chambersburg PA
CBHW051809100526
44592CB00016B/2623